# Valencia Travel Guide

*Attractions, Eating, Drinking, Shopping & Places To Stay*

Steve Jonas

# Table of Contents

Valencia ....................................................................................... 6

Planning Your Stay ............................................................... 13

Climate & Weather ............................................................... 15

Sightseeing ............................................................................... 17
    Cabacera Park & Valencia Bio Parc .............................. 17
    Cathedral ....................................................................... 19
    Silk Market (La Lonja de Seda) ................................. 20
    Central Market ............................................................. 22
    Serranos Towers .......................................................... 23
    City of Arts & Sciences ............................................... 23
    Hemisfèric Cinema ...................................................... 24
    Science Museum Príncipe Felipe .............................. 25
    Oceanogràfic Aquarium .............................................. 26
    Palau de les Arts .......................................................... 27
    Umbracle (City of Arts & Sciences) .......................... 28
    Ágora Events Arena ..................................................... 28
    Museum of Enlightenment & Modernity ................. 29
    Monastery San Miguel de los Reyes ........................ 29
    Palacio del Marques de Dos Aguas & Museo Nacional de
    Cerámica González Martí .......................................... 31
    Church of Saint John Hospital ................................... 32
    Almoina Archaeological Museum ............................. 33

Recommendations for the Budget Traveller ............. 34
    Places to Stay .............................................................. 34
        Purple Nest Hostel .......................................... 35
        Hotel Petit Germanias ...................................... 35
        Petit Palace Bristol Hotel ................................. 36
        Medium Hotels .................................................. 36
    Eating & Drinking ....................................................... 37
        Restaurante La Santa Compana ....................... 37
        Restaurante L'Estimat ...................................... 37
        Lambrusqueria .................................................. 38
        La Bodeguilla del Gato ..................................... 38
        L'Umbracle Terraza .......................................... 39

Casa Montana.................................................................................39
Carmen Neighborhood ...............................................................40
**Shopping** ........................................................................**40**
El Corte Ingles...............................................................................41
Calle La Pau & Calle Marques de Dos Aigue.........................42
Valencia F.C. Shop at the Train Station ................................42
Calle Don Juan de Austria & Calle Colon ..............................42
Teashop............................................................................................43

# Valencia

The Spanish city of Valencia has a curious charm all its own. There are remnants of ancient history dating back to 138 B.C. sitting next to ultra-modern buildings that have sprung up since the America's Cup was held here twice in the last few years.

Valencia never used to be high on the list of tourist destinations but took a sudden leap to fame when the America's Cup was held here in 2007 and again in 2010. Vast sums of money were invested in massive redevelopment programmes especially around the docks and marina which were transformed into attractive and tourist-friendly places to visit.

To the north of the docks and marina, the wide, flat beaches stretch for miles lapped by the clear blue Mediterranean Sea. The soft golden sands of Las Arenas, Cabañal and Malvarrosa are great places for families to visit. There are all the facilities needed for a great day at the beach with play parks for the children, toilets, shops and plenty of places to eat and drink. Most of the beachside restaurants (chiringuitos) have a BBQ or open fire blazing outside and the smell of sardines cooking as you walk past can be very tempting. Accompanied by a plate of salad the sardines make a tasty meal washed down with a glass of local wine. The tree lined promenade running alongside the beach is just right for a gentle stroll after a meal or just to soak up the sights and sounds of people having a good time.

There is something for everyone here and the city attracts not just holidaymakers but business travellers as well. Valencia is now is one of the leading cities in Europe for conferences and business fairs with facilities that are the envy of many places. If you are looking for designer shopping a good starting point is Calle Colón and the nearby streets where there is every brand name you could wish for. Leaving Calle Colón go towards the Plaza del Ayuntamiento and on to Barrio del Carmen in the Old Town where the shops become more individual and Spanish.

The Romans founded the city and the Old Town area around the Barrio del Carmen with its twisty narrow streets is a good place to start to find reminders of these ancient times. There is some beautiful architecture here amongst the brightly painted houses. Remember to take your time and look up at the buildings, some of the most striking architecture is often above street level. Most of these streets are too narrow for vehicles so watch out for mopeds hurtling round the corners.

There are plenty of bars and restaurants in the daytime but when nighttime comes it is just amazing how many more appear as if from nowhere. Doorways open to reveal tiny tapas bars sometimes with only one or two tables inside. Elsewhere shutters go up and the distinctive sound of flamenco music can be heard drifting through the streets mixed with disco. The Barrio is a cosmopolitan mix of every nationality and ethnic origin. The bars and clubs reflect this with places to suit all tastes, however wide and varied they may be.

In Spain nobody goes out 'early'. No self-respecting Spaniard would go out until at least 10pm and that is only if they plan on eating before making the most of the night time entertainment. In the hot summer months by midnight the streets surrounding the Plaza del Ayuntamiento will be full of couples of all ages wandering hand in hand, families enjoying a stroll in the cooler night air or just groups of friends wanting to chat over a few drinks.

The city of Valencia has many ancient buildings and historical sites that have stood for many hundreds of years and part of their attraction is the impact of time. The city is also full of modern architecture and one of the most striking buildings in Valencia stands on the site of the riverbed. The Turia River used to run through the city but the farsighted city designers realised that there was a better use for all this space and turned it into a park that now houses the City of Arts and Sciences. Designed by Santiago Calatrava and Félix Candelaat, construction started in 1996 with the final part of the project completed in 2005. The complex comprises a Science Museum, an IMAX cinema, the biggest aquarium in Europe, a multi-purpose venue and conference centre, plus an art and culture centre. A vantage point called the Umbracle is simply beautiful and is an area for walks, relaxation and taking in the views over the whole complex. There are various exhibitions held in and around this area and it also contains the Garden of Astronomy where much can be learnt about the stars.

Visitors to Valencia might be surprised to see many signposts and street names in not just Spanish (Castilian) but also in the local language (Valencian). It is a good idea to be aware of this although the Valencianos are not quite as sensitive to the linguistic issue as the people of Barcelona who feel even more strongly in favour of their native language of Catalan. Most people in Valencia speak Spanish as their first language these days with only some of the older residents being completely fluent in Valencian. Some of the younger people will have learnt English at school but it is still not that common to find fluent English speaking locals. Most English is spoken around the marina where the cruise ships come in.

Valencia is famous for being the birthplace of the well-known and much-loved Spanish dish called Paella. The Moors introduced the growing of rice to the area over a millennium ago and now several varieties are cultivated in the rice growing area of La Albufera. The growing of rice involves a year round painstaking process for the rice farmers who lovingly prepare the fields and then tend to their crops so we can benefit from these simple white grains.  In April the 3000 hectare Albufera lagoon along with the river Jucar floods over 14000 hectares of land which produces some 120 million kilos of rice every year.

As in many Spanish towns, many festivals are held during the year in and around Valencia. The one not to be missed is in March and is called Las Fallas and it features the most spectacular display of fire, music, dancing, pyrotechnics, fireworks and noise you will probably ever witness! Estimates as to how many visitors flock to see this deafening spectacle every year varies somewhere between two and three million people. The earth-shattering noise of the strings of mascleta firecrackers at 2pm each day of the festival can be heard and seen up close in the Plaza del Ayuntamiento and just about everywhere else as the whole city reverberates with the cannon-like explosions. The level of noise is such that pregnant women are actually discouraged from attending.

The Fallas themselves are huge sculptures made from wood and papier-mâché standing about 15 metres tall. These effigies can take the whole year to make and the current trend is to base them on celebrities and politicians. The festival starts on the 12th March and the Fallas are placed in the streets overnight on the 15th and 16th March. Leading up to the Fallas being displayed there are many bullfights, pageants, parades, competitions and much more to see and take part in.

Visitors can walk the city admiring each Falla while taking advantage of the many stalls serving food and drink and while listening to the music in a party-like atmosphere. On the stroke of midnight on the 19th March the Fallas go up in flames with more explosions being provided by fireworks hidden inside each one and then it is over for another year.

Huge paellas are cooked in the streets to feed the hungry crowds at Las Fallas by specialist companies in pans that can be up to several metres across. According to the Guinness Book of Records the largest Paella in the world was cooked by a Valencian in 1992 in a pan that measured 65 feet in diameter. It fed 110,000 people.

It would be wrong to not mention football when talking about Valencia. The successful Valencia C.F. team has a very strong following and has been the winner of the Spanish League and the UEFA Cup as well as UEFA Champions League runner up. The home stadium of Valencia C.F. is the Mestella where 55,000 fans can watch the beautiful game.

For a shopping experience visit one of the many markets. The Central Market is the place to go for fresh produce; the stalls are piled high with colourful and sometimes unusual foods while the vendors shout out what often sounds like unintelligible gibberish. Many of the stalls will have sample plates of their products to tempt you, so don't be shy and have a taste of fruit, cheese, fish, meat, ham, wines and sherries or whatever they might be offering. Even if you don't want to buy anything this market has to be visited just to admire the fantastic building it is housed in. From the outside it is quite hard to believe that anything as humble as a market could be inside such splendour. The arched windows and magnificent stonework are topped off by a spectacular dome which lets the light flood in to illuminate the 300 market stalls. It is not to be missed.

To visit a good car boot sale, head to El Rastro. You will definitely find some treasures amongst all the sometimes useless items, and if not it is also a good place to pick up some genuine souvenirs.

The Ruzafa market on Mondays is the place to go for cheap and cheerful clothes, toys, games, linen and other general market stuff. There is plenty to choose from, the quality might not be great but if you want something bright and colourful to wear to the beach it is a good place to go.

# Planning Your Stay

Valencia is located on the Costa del Azahar on Spain's Mediterranean coast which covers the 80 miles from Catalonia in the north to the Costa Blanca in the south. The self-governing region of Valencia is divided into three provinces, Alicante, Castellon and Valencia itself. Just below the halfway point on this stretch of coast, at the mouth of the Turia river (on the Gulf of Valencia) is the magnificent city of Valencia.

The Costa del Azahar is Spain's Orange Blossom Coast and a visit to the region in springtime makes it easy to see why. Orange groves full of trees with shiny green leaves and creamy white blossom stretch as far as the eye can see in this fertile land. By autumn the trees are dotted with bright orange as the fruits ripen ready to be picked. The fragrant scent of orange blossom is everywhere and it is a perfume that you will never forget.

In terms of population, Valencia is the third largest city in Spain with just over 800,000 inhabitants in the city and another million in the surrounding area. Valencia is equidistant from the other major cities of Barcelona and Madrid (both about 220 miles away) and Valencia is easily accessible by road and rail from both.

Valencia has two railway stations which are only ten minutes walk apart. Daily connections are available by rail from the Norte station in the heart of the city across not only Spain but also to Port Bou on the French/Spanish border. The newer Joaquim Sorolla station is used by the high speed and long distance trains to Madrid, Barcelona and Alicante. The AVE train to Madrid travels at 200 miles per hour.

The train service between Valencia Norte station and Valencia Airport runs from Monday to Friday every 30 minutes and the daily Aero-Bus service runs between the city and the airport every twenty minutes. Valencia (Manises) Airport lies to the west of the city and is the second busiest airport in the region after Alicante and the eighth busiest in the country. Flights from Valencia are available to many European airports as well as to North Africa and the Canary Islands.

Road connections to all of Spain are extensive with the AP-7 motorway running close to Valencia. The motorway runs the length of Spain and makes travelling from north to south easy and it provides a straight-through connection to France and the rest of Europe.  Madrid is easily accessible via the A-3.

For sauntering around the flat streets of Valencia there is a public bicycle rental service called Valenbisi. There are 250 bicycle stations around the city and tickets can be purchased at any of these on a daily or weekly basis.

The Port of Valencia is the largest port in Spain and the fifth busiest seaport in Europe. Due to its central location on the Mediterranean coast it is the second busiest container port in Spain and handles around 60 million tonnes of cargo a year. For many years it was a dull and unattractive industrial area, with hundreds of containers stacked up against a skyline of cranes and winches with not much else to recommend it. The only visitors to the area apart from the dock workers used to be travellers wishing to board the ferries to the Balearic Islands.

When Valencia was chosen by Switzerland to host the 2007 America's Cup a massive transformation of the dock area and the old marina began. The Juan Carlos 1 Marina was renovated and is now home to trendy bars and restaurants. The marina is to the east of the city next to the Las Arenas and Malvarrosa beaches. Cruise ships call in bringing passengers from all around the world eager to sample the delights that the centre of Valencia and the surrounding areas have to offer.

# Climate & Weather

Valencia has a great climate of long, warm to hot summers and mild winters. It has a sub-tropical climate and the summer season runs from April through until November.

The summer season is best for sunbathing when the daytime high can hit 34°C in August which is pleasant but not as meltingly hot as some of the more southern areas of Spain. The evenings are balmy and drop down to around 22°C which is ideal for dining al fresco at one of the many wonderful restaurants followed by a stroll along the promenade.

For a winter holiday January will be the coldest month, although that rather depends on your idea of cold. In the daytime the mercury hovers at 14°C but at night a chill sets in and the temperature can very quickly dip down sometimes as low as 2°C.

Spanish homes are not often equipped for cooler nights so warm night clothes are a good idea and tiled floors can be freezing to bare feet so socks or slippers are a must. Valencia is actually on the same latitude as Madrid yet the climates are very different. The temperature can drop well below freezing at night with sharp frosts and there are several ski areas just to the north of Madrid.

For sightseeing or a just a pleasant city break spring and autumn offer the best of everything. The temperature is mild, although it can rain, sometimes torrentially. Rain storms in the main are short and very heavy with water cascading down the street one minute and gone the next. Another advantage to not going in high season is that everywhere is generally less crowded, but if you choose the middle of March to visit watch out for the hoards that flock to Valencia for the Las Fallas festival. The spring months have an average high of 18°C with a low of 7°C, while the autumn figures are 23°C and 13°C. While this might feel warm to some people you can be sure the locals will still be wearing many layers of clothes.

The lucky Valencianos get more than their fair share of vitamin D each year as the yearly sunshine figures are 2,660, a whopping 70% more than the northern half of Europe. There is also more daylight with up to ten hours per day in the winter months with London or Moscow only getting around eight.

# Sightseeing

## Cabacera Park & Valencia Bio Parc

Avenida Pío Baroja, 3
46015 Valencia
Tel: +34 902 250 340
www.bioparcvalencia.es

In 2008 the Bioparc opened its doors to the public on the old Turia riverbed in the centre of Valencia.

Covering 25 acres within the Cabacera Park this innovative zoo has no apparent barriers so visitors feel like they are really out in the wild with the animals.

In their native Africa, right across the Savannah to Madagascar and Equatorial Africa, flora and fauna of many species co-exist and this has been recreated in Valencia. Elephants, leopards, hyenas, giraffes, hippopotamuses, lions, lemurs and ostriches are just a few of the species that live peacefully here side by side.

There are two snack bars within the Bioparc as well as a restaurant that serves a reasonably priced daily menu. Souvenirs and traditional African handicrafts can be purchased in the well-stocked gift shop. The Valencia BioParc is open every day of the year from 10am with the earliest closing being 6pm in the winter and slightly later in the summer. Admission prices are €24 per adult and €18 for children. There are concessions for students, groups and large families and children under the age of four get in free.

Cabacera Park itself is a great place for walks and there are some super photo opportunities from the special viewpoint. There is a lake where gentle trips on the water can be taken in boats shaped like giant swans which is great for families with children. As well as a bar and children's play area there is an open air auditorium where live performances are held.

# Cathedral

Plaza Almoina, s/n
46003
Valencia
Tel: +34 963 918 127
www.catedraldevalencia.es

Construction on the cathedral in Valencia started at the end of the 13th century and the building is predominantly Gothic although other architectural styles have been added. The cathedral has undergone several periods of renovation over its lifetime and currently is in remarkably good condition. The highlights inside the cathedral are the Chapel of the Holy Grail and the star motifs of the vault. Amongst numerous objects on display inside is a goblet from the first century AD, which is a relic from the Holy Grail.

Walking down the wide and airy nave leads you to the rather ornate but beautiful altarpiece with its Renaissance frescoes. On the outside the cathedral features two incredibly old doors, the Puerta del Palau is the oldest with Mudéjar elements in the Romanesque style and the Door of the Apostles is from the 15th century. The bell tower has eleven bells; some use an automated process to mark the hour and some can be rung manually. The bells in Valencia Cathedral are the largest group of Gothic bells in Spain.

In the Middle Ages King James I of Spain set up a council to administer the distribution of the water from the Turia river to local farmers. The council, Tribunal de las Aguas, survives to this day and the eight selected local farmers still meet every Thursday at midday at Valencia Cathedral. The meetings are in Valencian, the local language, and their word is law as far as irrigation and anything to do with the distribution of water goes. The Tribunal de las Aguas has been awarded the Intangible Cultural Heritage of Humanity by UNESCO.

The cathedral is open from 20th March until 31st October, Monday to Saturday from 10am to 6.30pm, Sundays and public holidays from 2pm to 6.30pm. From 1st November to 19th March, the hours are Monday to Saturday 10am to 5.30pm. The general admission price is €3 for adults and €2.10 for concessions. A guided tour is also available with audio guides available in many different languages.

# Silk Market (La Lonja de Seda)

Plaza del Mercado
46001
Valencia
Tel: +34 963 153 931

The building that houses the Silk Market in Valencia is considered to be the most beautiful Gothic building in the country and has been declared by UNESCO as a world heritage site.

This masterpiece of Gothic architecture doesn't give any clue from the outside as to the true nature of the business that was carried on inside. Many people think the building might be a castle as there is a huge tower; others think it maybe a church because of the ornately decorated door. Not many people would guess that that the origins of the building were as the local silk exchange.

During the 15th century the economy of Valencia was growing rapidly as the port meant that connections to other places in the world were relatively easy. The businessmen in the city needed somewhere to meet and make their deals according to their social status and so the Silk Market was built.

The vaulted ceiling in the main hall is supported by twisted columns which seem to stretch upwards forever from the marbled floor. The decoration is lavish and this style continues out into the garden with its orange trees and grotesque gargoyles. There are two other rooms in the compound and over the years these have served as courts as well as a prison and also as residences for city officials. In one of these rooms the tiling on the floor is intriguing and has an almost 3D effect.

Opening hours are Tuesday to Saturday 10am to 2pm and 4:30pm to 8:30pm, Sundays and public holidays 10am to 3pm and closed Mondays. Admission prices are €2 for adults and €1 for children and senior citizens.

# Central Market

Plaza del Mercado
46001
Valencia
Tel: +34 963 829 100
www.mercadocentralvalencia.es/

The Central Market will take your breath away as there are 400 hundred stalls spread out over two floors in this modern steel, glass and stone structure. Despite the modern materials the Central Market building is attractive with arched windows and doors and the roof is topped off with a central dome. The interior is big, bright and airy and well organised so everything is easy to find.

The stalls are laden with freshly picked and brightly coloured produce and it is easy to see why the Spanish shop daily with such bounty on their doorstep. The mingling smells of spices, exotic fruits and vegetables, fish, meats and flowers can be a heady perfume as you join in the hustle and bustle of the Valencianos doing their daily shopping. There are numerous tapas bars and cafeterias inside and outside the market building where after a busy morning of haggling it is great to have a coffee and watch the world go by.The market is open Monday to Saturday from 7am to 2pm.

# Serranos Towers

Plaza de los Fueros 46003 Valencia
Tel: +34 963 919 070

The Serranos Towers date from the Middle Ages and are one of twelve gates built as access points in the city wall. Designed by Pere Balaguer, a master stonemason, the actual gateway is a semi-circular arch with a pentagonal shaped structure either side. Only two of the twelve gates remain now and the Serranos Towers only survived the removal of the city wall in 1865 as they were in use as a prison for knights and noblemen. The towers are considered to be one of the landmarks of Valencia and are well worth a visit for their elegant Gothic style and sheer size. There are different levels which can be walked through all the way to the top from which there are stunning views across the city. The Serranos Towers are open Tuesday to Saturday from 10am to 6pm, with slightly longer hours in the summer. On Sunday and public holidays the gates open from 10am to 3pm but the admission is free. General admission is €2 and concessions pay just €1.

# City of Arts & Sciences

Avda. del Professor López Piñero & C/ Eduardo Primo
Yúfera 46013 Valencia
Tel: +34 902 100 031
www.cac.es/

The City of Arts and Sciences in Valencia is an amazing sight and to see all this complex has to offer can take more than one day.

The different areas of Hemisfèric, the Principe Felipe Science Museum, Oceangràfic, Palau de les Arts, Umbracle and Ágora offer opportunities to get to know the varying aspects of art, science, nature and technology.

In general the different areas open at 10am each day and close at 6pm, at weekends and in high season the closing times are slightly later. Each area has its own website link with admission prices and timetables of any special shows or performances. There is on-site car parking underneath the Umbracle but the public transport system is excellent with bus and train stops nearby.

There are plenty of places to eat and drink within the complex; pizzerias, burger bars, ice cream parlour's, a 750 seater self-service restaurant and the beautiful Submarino Restaurant where you can dine surrounded by 10,000 fish.

# Hemisfèric Cinema

www.cac.es/hemisferic/

For cinema lovers this is definitely the place to go. The concave screen is the largest in Spain and measures 900 square metres or nearly 3000 square feet. There is a varied timetable with films for children and adults, local information documentaries and nature programmes.

# Science Museum Príncipe Felipe

www.cac.es/museo/

This is a true 21st century science museum and uses didactic and interactive means to encourage visitors to understand our wonderful world of technology, science and the environment. Since its inauguration in 2000 over 27 million visitors have passed through its doors and been amused and surprised by this forward thinking museum.

The museum is on three floors, with the shops, restaurants and ticket offices on the ground floor. This level is free to the public and there are many exhibitions held in here each year.

On the first floor there are science exhibitions, many of which are interactive, and workshops where visitors can experiment with modules like "Exploratorium" and "Furnishing the World". A giant representation of a DNA helix can be seen as well as a Foucault Pendulum, one of the longest in the world at 110 feet. The pendulum is a simple device and demonstrates the rotation of the Earth.

From the top level of the museum there are spectacular views out over the Turia river park and children can have fun trying to count the 4,000 panes of glass that make up the museum building.

# Oceanogràfic Aquarium

www.cac.es/oceanografic/

Oceanogràfic in Valencia represents individuals from all of the world's main ecosystems and is the largest aquarium in Europe. In the Dolphinarium alone there are over there are 24 million litres of water. Across the whole site there are 500 different species: penguins, sharks, sea lions, turtles, manta rays, belugas, star fish, jelly fish and many others, as well as crustaceans of all types. Around 45,000 individuals swim, float and play in this aquatic environment.

The journey around the various buildings takes visitors past sheer glass walls where you can get up close and personal with the penguins and a walk through the glass tunnel where sharks swim overhead is almost as good as being in the water with them. There are examples of tropical mangrove swamps, and a bit closer to home, the Albufera de Valencia and its wetland bird species.

For those all-important souvenirs there are several gift shops in Oceanogràfic selling a variety of marine related items as well as sweets and snacks. In the Dolphin shop there are 500 products all with a dolphin theme and in the Arctic Bazaar the theme is penguins and Beluga whales as well as many other animals that call the Arctic and Antarctic home.

# Palau de les Arts

www.cac.es/palau/

The Valencia region has a privileged position in the world of culture and musical traditions and the Palau de les Arts has been constructed with this in mind. This modern space has the latest state of the art technology so whether you prefer to listen to opera singers or watch a ballet or enjoy a classical music performance, perfect sound is guaranteed.

Many major artists have performed here and a lot of these have been attracted by the leadership of Helga Schmidt who from 1973 to 1981 held a similar position at London's Royal Opera House. The Valencian Community Orchestra is the resident orchestra at the Queen Sofia Palace of the Arts and their first season was 2006-2007. Most seasons they perform seven or eight operas and a zarzuela. There are occasionally operettas and vocal recitals as well.

In 2007 Plácido Domingo bought his Operalia competition to Valencia and even now puts on regular performances. Opera galas, vocal recitals and symphonic performances are promoted by the Queen Sofia company and there is an advanced training programme for young artists. The Centre de Perfeccionament for these young people is named in honor of Plácido Domingo.

# Umbracle (City of Arts & Sciences)

www.cac.es/umbracle/

The Umbracle brings together all the areas of the City of Arts and Sciences and there are exhibition zones as well as walkways and lakes plus plenty of landscaped areas to sit and relax in. The Umbracle does a brilliant job in disguising the car park underneath and it is a pleasure to take a leisurely stroll and admire the fantastic vegetation representing the best that Mediterranean gardening has to offer.

Within the four or so acres of lush foliage and shady corners there is an Art Promenade with some very interesting sculptures by international artists. There is also a Garden Of Astronomy which complements the activities held in the Science Museum and this is an open access area for everyone to enjoy.

# Ágora Events Arena

www.cac.es/agora/

This multi-functional space is used for exhibitions, conferences, sports events, concerts and performances. Since its inauguration, various major events have been held at the Àgora including the Valencia Open 500 Tennis Tournament, Fashion Week and the Freestyle Burn Spanish Cup with both national and international riders taking part.

In the weeks leading up to Christmas there is plenty going on with a full programme of parties and shows for children plus an ice skating rink.

# Museum of Enlightenment & Modernity

Calle de Quevedo, 10, 46001 Valencia
Tel: +34 963 883 730
www.muvim.es

The Valencia Museum of Enlightenment and Modernity or MuVIM focuses on the history of media from the 17th century to the present day. There are permanent exhibitions as well as many temporary ones and workshops, courses, lectures and seminars are offered to complement these. There is a cafeteria, bookshop and shop and the opening times are Tuesday to Saturday 10am to 2pm and 4pm to 8pm, Sunday 10am to 2pm.

# Monastery San Miguel de los Reyes

Avinguda de la Constitució, 284
46019 Valencia
Tel: + 34 963 874 000
www.bv.gva.es/

A short distance from the city centre is this former monastery. It is built in the Renaissance style and the inner yard with its arches is a wonderfully tranquil place to rest awhile.

This beautiful building was built in the 16th century on the site of an old abbey and was looked after and loved until 1859. It was then used as a prison right up until the 1950's. A period of neglect followed until the monastery was restored and brought back into use.

The monastery sits in front of a marbled square, quite alone apart from a few gently waving palm trees. A visit here is an incredible experience which will leave a lasting impression, especially if the sun is setting during your visit casting a red glow across the beautiful stonework.

The building is now the headquarters of Valencia Library and home to the Valencian Language Academy, the Valencia Property Registry and the Directorate General of Books, Archives and Libraries.

A guided tour is available and this gives access to the church, crypt and the North wing. The guided tours are by prior appointment and are on Tuesday, Saturday, Sunday and public holidays. If you choose to wander alone access is restricted to the outside of this magnificent building and the South wing. The hours for this are Tuesday to Friday 10am to 2pm and 5pm to 8pm, Saturday, Sunday and public holidays 11am to 1.30pm. Admission is free as are the guided tours.

# Palacio del Marques de Dos Aguas &

# Museo Nacional de Cerámica

# González Martí

Calle del Poeta Querol, 2, 46002 Valencia
Tel: +34 963 516 392
www.mnceramica.mcu.es/

The Dos Aguas (Two Waters) in the name refers to Valencia's two main rivers and these are represented by two voluptuous male figures outside the door to this flamboyant Rococo palace. Along with these two oversized figures the main door is surrounded by the intricate alabaster carvings of fruit and vegetables.

Since 1954 the palace has housed the Ceramics Museum and this is an impressive collection where much can be learnt about the history of Valencia and its inhabitants. There is a Valencian kitchen where everything has been created out of ceramics and some fine examples of carriages that are so ornate it is hard to imagine them ever been used.

The admission fee for the palace and Ceramics Museum together is €3 for general entry and €1.50 for concessions. Entry is free on Saturday from 4pm to 8pm and on a Sunday. The opening times are Tuesday to Saturday 10am to 2pm and 4pm to 8pm. On Sunday and public holidays the hours are 10am to 2pm, closed all day Monday.

# Church of Saint John Hospital

Calle del Trinquete de Caballeros
46003 Valencia
Tel: +34 963 922 965
www.sanjuandelhospital.es

This historic church was constructed in the 13th century and was the first church to be built in the city after Valencia Cathedral. The land the church stands on was donated by James I and the Gothic and Baroque style church is dedicated to Saint John the Baptist. The site of the church used to be a hospital which is where the name comes from; the Jerusalem Order of the Hospital of Rhodes and of Malta.

The church has a single nave with chapels on either side and there are many 13th century frescoes and an interesting 16th century altarpiece. The church has suffered periods of neglect and has been lucky to survive demolition; it was only by the intervention of the Second Vatican Council that recovery work began. The work is still not completed and many thousands of Valencianos are supporting the restoration work with the aim of bringing the church back to its original splendour, some 700 years after it was first constructed.

The Prelature of Opus Dei are in charge of the church now and a full programme of worship is available as the church in general sees increasing activity in both interest and attendance levels. Services can be arranged in German, English and Dutch as well as Spanish.

The general opening hours are Monday to Friday 7am to 8am, 9.30am to 1.30pm, and 5pm to 9pm. Saturday 9.30 to 1.30pm and 5pm to 9pm and Sunday 11pm to 2pm and 5pm to 9pm.

# Almoina Archaelogical Museum

Plaza Decimus Junius Brutus (CONSOL Rome), s/n 46001 Valencia
Tel: +34 962 084 173

The Almoina Museum is fascinating as it has been built on the site where the ruins were discovered. Cleverly designed glass walkways protect the historical treasures that lie beneath but still allow visitors to see the wonders of this great find. The foundations that were uncovered have been left exactly as they were and a vast glass floor has laid over them so it is easy to get an understanding of the layout of the building exactly as it was two thousand years ago.

Many items of great historical significance have been found here and a tour of the museum gives an excellent insight into Valencia's history. Visitors can see the ruins of several ceremonial buildings, two Roman streets and a patio from an ancient Muslin city. There is an excellent example of a Roman spa from the 2nd century B.C. including a nearly complete Roman bath.

The entry fee of €2 is well worth it and if you choose to visit on a Sunday or public holiday between 10am and 3pm entry is free. The rest of the week the museum is open Tuesday to Saturday 10am to 6pm, with slightly longer hours in the summer months.

# Recommendations for the Budget Traveller

## Places to Stay

There is no shortage of cozy and budget-friendly places to stay in Valencia, no matter the season you decide to visit. Some will want to stay in the part of the city closest to the Cathedral, where the most shops, bars, and restaurants are concentrated, but you'll find Valencia extremely accessible even if you stay outside the Old City boundary. In any case, you'd be surprised how many places are affordable and can be found in close proximity to all the activities and main attractions.

# Purple Nest Hostel

The Purple Nest Hostel is one of the best budget-friendly hostels in the city, and boasts the largest communal kitchen in any of the hostels in Valencia. It is part of a chain, which helps in guaranteeing a certain level of service and also fairness in pricing. The beds and furniture are all relatively new, having been renovated in the last few years. As an added bonus, it is located right in the center of town, close to the Turia Gardens and main shopping and restaurant streets. Price for a night will vary according to season, but will not be more than 60 Euros.

Address: Plaza Tetuán, 5, 46003, Valencia
Telephone: +34 963 532 561
www.nesthostelsvalencia.com/purple

# Hotel Petit Germanias

Hotel Petit Germanias Valencia is a very affordable three-star boutique hotel which is located in the heart of Old Town. This hotel offers incredible value for your money, has free internet, and also has a bed-and-breakfast option that is very affordable. Prices, according to season, can range from 50-70 Euros per night, breakfast included.

Address: C/ Sueca, 14 46006 Valencia
Telephone: +34 963 513 638
http://www.hthoteles.com/es/hotel-petit-palace-germanias-valencia/

# Petit Palace Bristol Hotel

Petit Palace Bristol Hotel is located right next to the Cathedral, right in the center of Old Town. You would be hard-pressed to find a hotel with such high quality at such an affordable price. This hotel has free internet, some rooms with terraces, and a beautiful lounge where you can catch a drink before your big night out. You should expect to pay from 50-70 Euros per night here, depending on the season.

Address: Calle de la Abadía de San Martín, 3, Valencia
Telephone:  + 34 963 94 51 00
www.petitpalacebristolhotel.com/

# Medium Hotels

Medium Hotels is a chain of moderately priced hotels in Spain. The Medium Hotel in Valencia has more than 150 rooms, a pool, free wifi, and several lounges and breakfast rooms. There's also a Mediterranean restaurant right on the premises, in case you're too tired to hop outside and traipse around town. This hotel is also special because it has several promotions that you can opt for on its website, including all-inclusive packages with breakfast or tours. You may even want to choose the "Bicycle" package to tour around Old Town on a bicycle for three hours one morning. Expect to spend around 50-70 Euros per night, depending on the season.

Address: General Urrutia, 48, 46013
Telephone: +34 963 34 78 00
https://www.mediumhoteles.com/

# Eating & Drinking

Come to Valencia, and you will not go hungry. From fresh fish plucked from the Sea to huge portions of Paella prepared slowly over a low heat, you will not be disappointed at the culinary variety you will find here. Here are some places not to miss.

# Restaurante La Santa Compana

Restaurante La Santa Compana is a great choice for a wide variety of food, not just your local fare. Expect to come here and enjoy a juicy steak, or other specials the chef may decide to whip up. This restaurant also boasts an *enoteca*, a section of the restaurant you can order a more casual meal with some delicious local wine. Price: 20 Euros per person.

Address: Calle Roteros 21, El Carmen, Valencia
Telephone: +34 963922259

# Restaurante L'Estimat

Restaurante L'Estimat is the place to get your Paella.

To get the best "local" experience, go at lunchtime where you'll share a table and maybe even a dish or two with the residents. There are other fresh dishes to choose from, and you won't be disappointed with the seafood, or the view. This treasure is located right on the sea. Price: 20-30 Euros per person.

Address: Avda. Neptuno 16, Playa de las Arenas, Valencia
Telephone: +34 96 371 10 18
http://www.restaurantelestimat.com/eng/index.htm

# Lambrusqueria

Lambrusqueria is the place to go for Mediterranean food of the Italian variety. It's tucked away in the center of town, and has both indoor and outdoor seating. Even though their specialties include pasta and salad, you'll also want to try some Tapas for some local flair.

Address: Calle Conde Altea 31,Valencia
Telephone: +34 963340753
http://lambrusqueria.wordpress.com/

# La Bodeguilla del Gato

La Bodeguilla del Gato serves perhaps the best Tapas in town.  Walk into this small bodega and you are bathed in the brightest orange walls you've ever seen – smothered with everything from Renaissance paintings, wooden spoons, and a bicycle.  Go and expect to order a lot more than you originally planned, as the menu is just that good.  Open until 2 am, you may end up staying for more than the food, as the atmosphere gets more relaxed and vibrant as the night goes on. At the weekend, plan on calling ahead to make a reservation.

Address: Calle de Catalans, 10
46001, Valencia
Telephone: +34 963 918 235

# L'Umbracle Terraza

Spend all day in the City of Arts and Sciences?  Don't think you need to get back to city center or the beach to have a good time.  One of Valencia's best new bars is here, and has a great variety of tapas, cocktails, and a gorgeous terrace where you can dance the night away.

Address:  Avda. del Saler 5,
City of Arts and Sciences, Valencia
Telephone: + 34 607 659 705
http://www.umbracleterraza.com

# Casa Montana

After dinner, head down to this small, cozy wine and cocktail bar for some drinks before hitting the town. It is known for its excellent Spanish wine collection, and the bartenders are the perfect balance of knowledgeable and modest. Seats fill up quickly, but it's equally fun to be up at the beautiful wooden bar, watching the bartenders work their magic.

Address: Calle de José Benlliure, 69, Valencia
Telephone: + 34 963 67 23 14
www.emilianobodega.com

# Carmen Neighborhood

If you're looking for a night out you certainly will never forget, look no further than within the confines of the old city, in the old, winding streets behind the Cathedral. This is where you can best experience the melting pot of Valencia for yourself, as everyone, no matter your race, age, class, or creed, finds a bar or club to hang out here. It is definitely the "alternative neighborhood" of Valencia, but the variety of locals it offers has something for everyone.

For the most bars and clubs, head to the area between the Torres de Serranos and the Plaza de la Virgen; this is where the nightlife is most concentrated. While many bars and clubs will be absolutely worth your while, you may want to try out **Radio City, Pinball, Mitjanit, and Bigornia** as some of the local favorites. Most of these clubs close at around 4 am, so be prepared to close up and head to the beach, or into Carmen for some late-night action.

For a complete listing of clubs and bars, go here: http://www.valenciavalencia.com/nightlife-guide/carmen/carmen-nightlife.htm

## Shopping

Whether you're in Valencia for the beautiful beaches, for the tapas, for the Flamenco, or for the dusk-till-dawn nightlife, you'll absolutely need a break to shop. Or at least you should take a break to shop, whether for a ripe orange or for a new pair of Manolos, as this town has more shops you can visit in a lifetime.

While you're here, though, best to follow the local daily schedule, and expect shops to be closed during most of the afternoon hours, particularly from 1pm to around 4 or 5pm. This is when the town takes a *siesta*, or afternoon nap, and you should too, if you plan on having the night you should here.

Valencia is like many Spanish towns, where many stores are clustered along several streets or in a certain neighborhood. The following is a list of some great places to start. Of course, the best way to find your favorite shop is to get lost: wander in the alleyways behind the cathedral, along the old riverbed and the ancient walls of the city. You'll be surprised what treasures you may find.

# El Corte Ingles

This Spanish institution is a one-stop-shop for just about anything you want to find from a department store. Need an extra bathing costume for the beach? Need to pick up a new pair of shoes, or sunglasses? Head to one of this store's many locations to pick up whatever you might need for a great price. Check the website for the most convenient store to your location: http://www.elcorteingles.es/

# Calle La Pau & Calle Marques de Dos Aigue

These two streets in the center of town are the places to go if you fancy shopping local names like Carolina Herrera, and also the international design super-stars like Prada or Versace. These streets can be a bit more expensive but if you search you will find a bargain hidden in the designer aisles. These streets are also ideal if your idea of a perfect afternoon is window-shopping and people-watching: the designs you'll see even just walking down these streets will make your eyes pop.

# Valencia F.C. Shop at the Train Station

Your eyebrows may be raised, but this is the place to go to buy your Valencia F.C. Merchandise. Inside the train station is city's official store to find anything in support of the local football club.

# Calle Don Juan de Austria & Calle Colon

These are the best streets to wander down if you're not too into the designer scene but you're more into the mid-range stores like H&M, Desigual, and Mango. These two streets run into each other, so if you hit one, you're not far from the other.

# Teashop

If you want to get your friends and family a unique gift, stop by this boutique store to buy any assortment of tea, or create your own special blend. The shopkeepers are nice and welcoming, and are in no way snobbish about their teas, so ask away, and come away with a souvenir that will last you months to come.

Address: Calle de Jorge Juan, 1, Valencia
Telephone: 963 517 722
http://www.teashop.es/

15496123R00028

Printed in Great Britain
by Amazon